Finding Purpose

Manifesting A Ble:

Life Planning

GOD'S WAY

Andrea L. Hudson-Johnson

Life Planning God's Way

Trilogy Christian Publishers A Wholly Owned Subsidiary of Trinity Broadcasting Network

2442 Michelle Drive Tustin, CA 92780

Rights Department, 2442 Michelle Drive, Tustin, CA 92780.

Trilogy Christian Publishing/TBN and colophon are trademarks of Trinity Broadcasting Network.

For information about special discounts for bulk purchases, please contact Trilogy Christian Publishing.

Trilogy Disclaimer: The views and content expressed in this book are those of the author and may not necessarily reflect the views and doctrine of Trilogy Christian Publishing or the Trinity Broadcasting Network.

Manufactured in the United States of America

10 9 8 7 6 5 4 3 2 1

Library of Congress Cataloging-in-Publication Data is available.

ISBN: 978-1-68556-292-2
E-ISBN: 978-1-68556-293-9

DEDICATION

I dedicate this book to those who believe that there is an untapped purpose that is tied to success on the inside of them and who are truly determined to find their God-given purpose in life so that they can head to destiny.

ACKNOWLEDGMENTS

This book would not be possible if I did not have key persons in my corner to support, encourage, edify, empower, and pray for and with me during my winter season of experiencing one of my greatest hardships in life.

To my spiritual mother, Essie Ware, thank you for praying and prophesying the Word of God over my life. You have reminded me of God's plan for my life on many occasions. I thank you so very much for exhorting me with the words in which God placed on your heart that have propelled me to go to my next level in Christ.

To my friends, Lashebra Morgan, Pamela Thomas Webb, and Morgan Lopez, I thank God for blessing me to have bonus sisters in Christ that I had to lean on so many days that seem to be too dark to walk through and too weak to stand. I am so blessed to know that I have a few good women in my corner to push me with the Word of God.

To my grandmother, mother, father, and four sisters (Kimberly,

Josephine, Vosheena, and Japonica), every minute, every hour, and every day, you were there. I felt the most love from you all during my most difficult time in life. Thank you for the unlimited love and compassion that was given to me when I needed it the most. Family is truly everything.

To my three children, Jemerion, Mikevious, and Mikyon: God couldn't have blessed me any more than when He saw fit for me to birth such gifts into this world. The glory of the Lord is truly upon you. My life is so heavenly blessed because of you. I know that there is a great plan and calling on your lives, and God is going to use you all mightily in His kingdom. You will forever be my "mighty men of God."

To my husband, Kentrell Johnson, thank you so much for loving me back to life. You are my rock and my greatest support during this whole process. You created such a loving environment for me to grow and flourish and become better to you, for you, and with you as a partner. Thank you for believing in me even when things appeared still and void. Thank you for the love, the push, the support, and the many nights that you have allowed me to talk your ear off about finding purpose and heading to destiny. I love you.

I give all the glory, the honor, and the praise to my Heavenly Father for downloading such word down on the inside of me to give to those who are ready to experience the grace that God has promised to all who receive Him. All God wants is a yes, and He will align your life with the ultimate plan He gave you when you were in your mother's womb. It was God who equipped me, empowered me, and edified me to find my purpose so that I may head to destiny by fulfilling His plan in which He has plainly laid out for me step by step. All glory belongs to the King of Kings and the Lord of Lords, God Almighty.

TABLE OF CONTENTS

SYNOPSIS

How do you plan to live your life? Your way or God's way?

Balancing life can seem so hard to grip. Between your spouse, the kids, extended family, work, meetings, etc., it's hard to find your next breath, let alone find time for yourself.

Life Planning God's Way lays out a simple version of how to navigate through life by implementing God's Word. Your life has a definite purpose tied to it, and when you invite God into it, it's going to shift you on the path of pursuing the vision that God has customized for you.

Your purpose, your destiny, fulfillment, and abundance are on the horizon. Balancing life will be in the palm of your hand.

INTRODUCTION

A small-town girl with big dreams! That's me, Andrea Hudson. I was born in a very small town in Mississippi by the name of Sherard. I am the second born of four sisters. Coming up where I lived, your only option was to *dream big*. Surrounded by cotton fields and gravel roads, I lived with my grandmother, who was the sole provider of the house. My mom, oldest sister (only sister at the time), five uncles, and aunt all lived in one small tin-top home made of wood and what looked like sandpaper covering the exterior of our home. My grandmother's occupation was picking cotton for a few dollars a day to provide for all of us. I guess my struggle is what motivated me to *dream big*. Although dreaming big was but a mere illusion, I knew it had to be more to it as I got older.

It wasn't until my early adult years when I began to believe that there was something different about me. I have always stood out from the crowd. My introverted personality did not provide me much of an advantage because I was mostly a loner. Crowds were never a thing for me, and I was always alright with that position.

Being alone was an energy booster, and I was most productive and creative in my thinking when it was just me and no one else within my personal space. This is how my spiritual identity came into play later. I was more intuitive with who I was as an individual, and I knew that I was a peculiar kind. I was birth to be different. My routine was very different from other individuals. I ran my life by a schedule starting at the age of fourteen. From my schooling to my extra-curricular activities, working out, etc. I was alone so much to where my time and tasks had to be strictly managed, or I will become unproductive and depressed. I had to stay busy enough to be productive and, on the other hand, allow myself downtime to process my feelings and understand where I was mentally. "Me" time.

Ultimately, I became very reserved and was not interested in surrounding myself with many people earlier on in my life because my dialogue and level of intellect were stretched so far from an average mind to where I was misunderstood on so many levels. I had a few people I called friends, which was a high executive position in my life because these were those who understood me, and I trusted them with the most valuable pieces of information of me, and I knew that if I told them anything classified, it remained classified. I wasn't a secretive (having concealed intentions) individual. I was just more on the sacred (protected and secure) side of things. I was a person of divine value, which was for me to cultivate relationships that were like-minded.

I am known as a radical risk-taker. I am not afraid of anything. If I wanted something, I prayed about it, and then I pursued it. I have many life stories about this part of my life, but just to name a few, I left many secured jobs to pursue my own endeavors in business, I moved from city to city in pursuit of my own happiness, and I wasn't afraid to begin again after heartbreak in relationships. However, I failed so many times in each area, but that's the ideal point of taking a risk.

Now, I must remind you, risk-taking plus failing should always equal out to making a wiser decision when taking the next risk. My method of course-correcting my risks in which I failed was to analyze and identify what went wrong, recalculate the equation, then come up with another solution. I was a critical thinker who solely believed in taking calculated risks. My strongest personality traits were that of me being self-motivated, systematic, and highly optimistic. When I failed, I got back up and tried it again. My entire life and being revealed the glory of God who lives within me to keep moving in faith and persistence. Abraham from the Bible scriptures is who I have always compared my life with because Abraham was a man of faith! He moved when God said to move. He made an alter everywhere he went. He didn't mind sending sacrifices up to God because his faith in God was very strong. He was patient in his waiting when God gave him a promise, and he solely depended on God to answer every prayer.

On the other hand, Abraham had a side of him that caused him to make his own decisions at times without consulting God. His unfavorable circumstances sometimes wore in on him and motivated him to move in his own will, which later caused heartache and pain, but yet God still favored Abraham withholding none of His blessings and promises because Abraham was a man of *faith* and *prayer*. Abraham's faith moved God, and his prayers were honored because he always acknowledged God in all of his ways. God had mercy on Abraham when he made a move without consulting Him because Abraham had a personal relationship with God causing favor to fall in Abraham's life.

In essence, my life began to make sense after I read the story of Abraham because our lives were so similar and his relationship with God prompted me to develop my own personal relationship with God. I viewed Abraham's life as a blueprint for my own life. I always reverted to the story of Abraham to see how he handled situations when I was in one. In that, me seeking God through a man in which God so highly favored turned into a present moment revelation of God Himself speaking to me in a fresh way.

This is how God works if you provide Him the space to come in and work your life. Faith moves God! After seeking God on so many occasions, God gave me clarity (vision) on the blessings He had for me. He revealed to me my life's purpose and plan and how He wanted me to operate in it. In my prayer time, He downloaded in me His plan of how He wanted me to operate on the earth for His purpose. Purpose requires practical faith in God, balance, and order. God does not want us to be double-minded and without vision, so He gives us His plan of how to be fruitful and multiply in abundance if we seek Him and acknowledge Him in all of our ways.

Now, I understand that God provided His plan only to prosper me as long as I serve His purpose for my life. It is the same for you. You are here on this earth for a reason. You were not a mistake. There is something you were birth here to do and in order to understand your life and your purpose, turn the page.

1.

THE ULTIMATE VISION

"Where there is no vision, the people perish..."

(Proverbs 29:18, KJV).

As a child, I always did things that eventually manifested into who I am and what I am striving to do in the future. The little motivation that surrounded me enabled me to dream big, which later became my vision. God wants to download in you your next move. He is more concerned with the finished works in your life, which is known as the ultimate vision.

Your vision and plan are not God's vision and plan. God sees you in a much broader lens, and if you take the time to provide a space for God to come in and have His way in your life, He will show you: "'What no eye has seen, what no ear has heard, and what no human mind has conceived'—the things God has prepared for those that love him—" (1 Corinthians 2:9).[1] You are going to be so much bigger and better than what your circumstances reveal to you if you seek

---

1 Jimmy Swaggart, The Expositor's Study Bible (Baton Rouge, LA, 2005, 2010).

Him.

Every area of your life will be to grow and prosper into something that you could not see for yourself because it will be God's end result for you. His end result for you will be an increase, healing, prosperity, abundance, and protection. His favor is going to overtake you and overflow your cup. His vision and plan will open doors no man can close and close doors no man can open. The business in which you see for yourself is nothing compared to how big God can make it. The relationships you desire don't compare to the divine relationships God has set up for you. They will be for you and not against you. Your financial situation is but a small thing to God. Just ask, and you shall receive because, with God, all things are possible! He will make every situation that looks like a failure in your life and turn it into a miraculous winning situation.

All things are possible to those who believe. Just believe that the vision God has for your life is the beginning of who God envision you to be. You are not who you were yesterday because the Bible says, "Therefore if any man be in Christ, he is a new creature: old things are passed away; behold, all things are become new" (2 Corinthians 5:17, KJV). That means God is going to give you fresh and new relationships with like-minded people; your finances are going to increase, you will become "whole" spiritually, mentally, physically, and emotionally, you will get your dream job, your entrepreneurial endeavors are going to expand because you made the decision to seek God in a new way. The vision God has for you is greater than your own eyes can see and much greater than your own mind can imagine.

In Genesis 12:1–3, God spoke to Abraham for the first time, telling him to go from his country, his people, and his father's house to the land in which I will show you. He told Abraham that He would make him into a great nation, and He will bless him. God said to him that He will make his name great, and he will be a blessing; that He will bless those that bless him and curse those that curse him, and all people on earth will be blessed through Him.

Abraham had a relationship with God. He was able to recognize the voice of God when God spoke out about the ultimate vision which was laid out for his life. Abraham received the vision, and then he moved in the vision with no questions asked. When God gives you the vision, you have to be like Abraham and move in it. Abraham trusted the Word of God when God told him to leave the land without exactly knowing where he was going. He *walked by faith*. This is a message for you to understand when God gives you the vision; you just have to move in it. You don't need to see everything right off. Just move because if God gave you the vision, it is God's responsibility to lead you and guide you in it. That's the purpose of faith. Your faith will enable God to give you the next step. Then, the next step. God wants you to depend on Him and Him alone.

When God spoke to me about my vision, I was in a very depressed and lame state in my life. Hope was my state of mind in spite of what my situation looked like. I was persistent because I believed that there was greater for me. Finally, after high school, I enrolled myself in cosmetology school, and this is where I was in life when God began to speak to me about my vision. The higher I went in this industry, the plainer the vision became. This very thing dropped me off at the corner of my life plan and goals. See, if God gives you the vision, He is going to give you the steps to go with it. My faith in God stretched because I had to lean and depend on Him to get each step. One day, God spoke again. I was prompted in my spirit to create a life plan. This life plan was laid out with goals and the action plan that God used as an instrument to see the vision fulfilled. This was God's way of providing me with my next steps. I became very nervous and began to wonder, How is this even possible? God led me to just believe, trust, and have faith in what he promised me. I had to write down the vision on paper as God had given it to me. As time passed, God added to my vision because His plans were to prosper me past what I could see for myself. I kept my notepad and pen on hand because I could not afford to miss what God was going to speak to me about my vision. I stayed in the spirit of expectancy.

...if God gives you the vision, He is going to give you the steps to go with it.

When you are in pursuit of the vision, there will be tough encounters and look like situations that will challenge you along the way. I call it the lies of life. If it doesn't look like what God said to you about your vision, it is called "the lies of life." One thing about life, in general, you must understand is whether it is the truth or lie; life will only manifest only how you see it. The Bible says, "So as a man thinks in his heart, so is he" (Proverbs 23:7). If life is presenting the opposite of what the vision is, this is where you allow God to show up and handle it. The Bible also says, "Be still and know that I am God" (Psalm 46:10). When God gave you the vision, the opposition was factored in it. This is why God shows you the end of a thing at the beginning because God is the Alpha of your vision and the Omega of your vision, and He wants you to stay hopeful of the vision in which He, Himself, has given you. The "in-between" is God's battle, not yours. Your responsibility is to walk by faith and not by sight. God will allow you to trod down dark pathways of life only to strengthen you in your faith. You cannot discover your full potential and purpose in life without trials and tribulations. God had a plan for it all. You have to keep pushing and keep believing in the vision in which God has given you.

Abraham encountered some of the toughest situations life offered, but he never gave up. In Genesis 12:9, Abraham and his family encountered a famine in the land which, in his own will, decided to temporarily live in the land of Egypt until the famine passed. In spite of Abraham's decision to go to Egypt to survive, God had mercy on Abraham and his family. Abraham was gifted grace and mercy from God because he had a relationship with God. Abraham needed grace and mercy when he moved out of the will of God because that move was not a part of the plan. He moved out of the will of God when he decided to move to Egypt, told his wife, Sarai, to lie to the Egyptians, saying that Abraham was her brother just to spare his life. Sarai ended up marrying Pharaoh, which was not the vision God gave Abraham. Verse 17 said that the Lord inflicted diseases on Pharaoh and his household because of Sarai, Abraham's wife, just to get out of the situation they put themselves in. How many times have you messed up and God delivered you out? Thank God for His sufficient grace. The Bible says in 2 Corinthians 12:9 (ESV), "And he said unto me, 'My grace is sufficient for you, for my power is made perfect in weakness.'" When there seemed to be no way out for Abraham and his family, God's grace is how they were delivered out of Egypt.

Many times in life, your current situation will reveal the lies of life, which motivates poor decisions making. These are all hindrances that stagnate you from pursuing the vision. Trials and tribulations will present false images about your life and serve as a device of the enemy to set you in the opposite direction of where God has intended for you to travel. Zero in on your vision in stillness and quietness, and God will download your next move. Just believe.

You have to keep pushing and keep believing in the vision in which God has given you.

Journal Writing Exercise

Your Ultimate Vision

Name:

Date:

Writing your vision brings so much clarity and direction into your life. No matter where you are, there is always hope. For this exercise, write down where you would like to be in three years, five years, ten years.

2.

THE PURPOSE OF YOUR VISION

"And we know that all things work together for good to
them that love God, to them who are called according to
his purpose"

(Romans 8:28, KJV).

We all have a reason for being. God has placed us on the
earth to live out the purpose He has put in us. There is a
definite purpose for your life. This is a phrase in which I've heard
throughout my life, and I know it to be true. God wants you to
write the vision down on paper. Vision comes from God and God
alone. A vision is simply a power of sight downloaded within you
from heaven. This heavenly download is the creative idea from God
in the form of a vision that gives you a sense of direction in your
life. If you can see it, then you can achieve it. Writing it down holds
you accountable for going after the vision.

When you begin to pursue the vision for your life, God will
provide a vehicle that will drive you to operate in your purpose.

Your purpose for having a vision is for you to live a happy, healthy, wealthy, abundant, and fulfilled life as the Lord wants you to live. The Bible says, "You will lend to many nations but will borrow from none. The Lord will make you the head, not the tail…you will always be at the top, never the bottom" (Deuteronomy 28:12–13, NIV). "No, in all these things we are more than conquerors through him who loves us" (Romans 8:37, NIV). The vision God gives you will affect other lives that are connected to you. There is a group of people who are waiting on you to step out in faith to help pull them out of the same struggles in which you have overcome. You have the blueprint to help them. Your purpose will help set the captives free, and the only way to do it, you must *write the vision.* Ask God to give you the vision. When the vision is on paper, the vehicle of purpose will arrive. Your purpose is in what you do every day. It's your flow, that thing you do so easily. Your passion is your purpose! Your passion is the vehicle that will help you to attain and live in the vision in which you have written down. It takes an everyday pulling on God to get your next steps.

Seeking God for your purpose is key, and God will give you great clarity that will empower you to go after the vision in which He has set for your life. Creating a vision and knowing the purpose for your vision will steer you in the direction of success and will cause your success to pour onto others in your reach. Moreover, when you are in pursuit of the vision, there will be many obstacles that will fall on your path. Trials and tribulations come to make you stronger in your mind so that you can continue to overcome the struggles ahead. Anything that is hard is worth having.

So, you must keep going and stay focused on the reason and purpose of your vision. The vision is the end goal. The purpose of your vision is the motivation to keep it moving. You have to believe that all things are working for your good. Affirm every day to yourself, "I can do all things through Christ [Jesus] who strengthens me" (Philippians 4:13, NKJV). God is an intentional God, and He will never put too much on you. If He placed it in your path, He has already given you the power to overcome it.

Allow God to reveal His glory through you by focusing on His vision for your life. Understand that the vision God gives you has a purpose, and with His leading (the Holy Spirit) and His power down on the inside of you, you will achieve it all.

Journal Writing Exercise

The Purpose of Your Vision

Name:

Date:

There is a purpose in everything, even your vision. Ask yourself, "Why is my vision so important?" For this exercise, write down the importance of your vision and how you plan to impact others with your vision.

3.

AREAS OF LIFE TO FOCUS

"Now may our Lord Jesus Christ Himself and God our Father,
who has loved us and given us eternal comfort and good hope
by grace, comfort and strength your hearts in every good work
and word"

(2 Thessalonians 2:16–17, NASB).

Balance brings peace of mind by the Lord Himself that surpasses all understanding in our lives. Life has its way of bringing the flow of busyness in our direction to wear it sometimes causes us to lose track of ourselves. It often throws you off balance in every area of your life if you are not careful enough to slow down and give equal attention to your areas of life to focus. The Bible makes it plain that God is a God of order, and He expects us to duplicate His ways in order to live fulfilled.

How must you balance? Well, first, it is important to categorize your areas of life to focus on, along with creating goals and action plans for each area. Having goals for each area of your life brings about an awesome balance. This was extremely challenging for me, in the beginning, to tend to these areas of my life without setting goals and creating action plans to accommodate these areas.

After I decided to make time to get it together, it became a life-changing experience. It takes strict discipline. I sat down with my pen and paper and wrote down the top five most important areas of my life. Then, I began to set SMART goals for each area. A SMART goal is an acronym that gives criteria to guide you in setting objectives for your areas of life to focus on. Simply put, your goals must be Specific, Measurable, Attainable, Relevant, and Time-Based. Once you have completed this, you will feel a sense of relief because now, you have clarity as to how you will execute your way through.

My areas of life to focus has a lot to do with something I call "the Hat Theory." The Hat Theory is how I compartmentalize each area of my life by creating action plans to meet each goal success-fully on a time/task management basis. Your role at hand is deter-mined by the hat in which you put on at that moment and is im-portant for the purpose of bringing a balance to each area of your life. Prioritizing your tasks on paper gives you a clear vision of how you should execute each area. In this, a major factor to consider is that of an action plan. Why? Because for you to compartmentalize and improve those areas of your life, you must first create an action plan to fulfill them. The hat in which you are wearing at that moment in time will help you to stay compartmentalized and focused on the task at hand. Your life will balance and flow so easily when you operate in what I call "the Hat Theory."

Allow me to present to you a blueprint of how you may balance out your areas of life to focus on and how stylishly and strategically you may wear your hats in each role. Keep in mind: you must make constant adjustments because things are always changing. You will find it quite easy to make the necessary changes needed because of what's already in place. Areas of life to focus on and action plan is as follows:

1. Relationship Area: Marriage, Kids, Family, Friends
   o Action Plan
     • Marriage: Date once a week/spend quality time x hour(s) a day, cook x times a week, submit to his areas of needs daily, buy unexpected appreciation gifts once a week, getaways once a month.

     • Children: Spend time regularly, regular family outings x times a month, get actively involved at their school, give more hugs and kisses daily, reaffirm and show love daily.

     • Family and Friends: Call once x times a week, visit x

times monthly, send occasional gifts of appreciation on birthdays and Christmas.

2. Finances
   o Action Plan
     - Give charitably often; track and manage daily, weekly, and monthly spending; save/invest % per paycheck; spend wisely.

3. Education
   o Action Plan
     - Pursue your higher education/diploma/certification, attend business workshops and seminars x times a year, obtain necessary certifications, licenses, and other credentials.

4. Business
   o Action Plan
     - Self-appraisal process, organize business ownership, meet requirements locally and state-wise; seek proper advisers before operations: accountant, insurance agent, distributors, attorneys, etc.

5. Spiritual

   o Action Plan

      • Prayer/meditation/fasting schedule; attend and get active in the church.

6. Health

   o Action Plan

      • Eat more organic fruits and veggies, eat full meals moderately, drink plenty of water, exercise regularly, practice saying no, schedule my daily tasks, rest x hours a day, self-care x times monthly.

Your role at hand is determined by the hat which you put on at that moment, and it is important for the purpose of bringing a balance to each area of your life.

When you discover your top five areas of life to focus on, design your SMART goals and action plans on how to accomplish order in each area. I must tell you that this is a project that requires time. You may decide to figure out your areas of life to focus on today. Tomorrow you may pick up on your goals. The next day, you may work on your action plan. You must do what works for you. The end goal is to get it done. The ups and downs of life have shown me how to bring forth a balance to each area of my life by paying close attention to what was off and simply fixing it.

Know this: God has ways of speaking to you daily about your life. Just be still and know that He is God. He will clearly show you how to bring a balance to your life, just as He has shown me. For you to live a happy life, you must, first, develop the desire to want balance, discovering what areas of your life in which you would need to focus. Then simply create a plan for those areas in which you have chosen to work on. Break them down into SMART goals and action plans/objectives. Then, trust God to bring it all together. You will be well on your way to live a happy, healthy, and wealthy life. God's love for you will give you everlasting consolation in every area of your life. Choosing to allow Him into your life will make all crooked places straight, and anything in your life you may find disorderly, He will bring divine order. Decide today. The best is yet to come.

Journal Writing Exercise

Areas of Life to Focus

Name:

Date:

Balance is an essential part of life. Without it, we find ourselves burned out and living in chaos. For this exercise, write down five areas of your life that need attention. Then, write SMART goals and an action plan with a timeline of when you want to accomplish each goal.

4.

YOUR IDENTITY

"Nay, in all these things we are more than conquerors
through him that loved us"

(Romans 8:37, KJV).

It is in your darkest hour when the enemy creeps into the crevices of your mind and whispers lies about you and your life. He doesn't play fair. See, the enemy is very clever, and he thoroughly studies us 360 degrees. He knows how to trigger your negative emotions, which causes you to fall into negative thoughts about yourself and your life. Your identity is his very target. If you forget who you are in Christ, you will begin to take on a false identity. One less powerful and less than who you were born to be. *How can you reclaim your true identity?* You reclaim your true identity by speaking what the Bible says about you, affirmations that awaken you to your true self.

The Bible says in 1 Peter 2:9 (KJV), "But ye are a chosen generation, a royal priesthood, an holy nation, a peculiar people; that ye should shew forth the praises of him who hath called you out of darkness into his marvelous light." Life will take you down many pathways and place you in environments that will rob you of who you truly are. You will soon begin to pick up false behaviors and false attitudes, which will encourage you to believe the lie of the enemy about yourself. It will make you believe that this is your final result. Unfortunately, life lies to you in so many ways, and it is in your weakest and darkest hour the enemy creeps in and whispers to you his lies to keep you trapped in a stagnated position.

Don't believe the lies. Life left me in a rut on many occasions. In all honesty, my decisions to settle made me stay in those ruts longer than I needed to. Because I settled, I suffered physical abuse, emotional abuse, and mental abuse time after time after time again by those who said they loved me. My hurt caused me to hurt others that were for me because I did not know how to love anymore. Life would not let up on me because I did not know who I was. I clearly had an identity crisis. I was bound by generational curses, depression, and low self-esteem. My self-worth and confidence were shot. I was hopeless. This detriment led me to become very rebellious and careless, which dug me into a deeper rut.

At this point in my life, I could not trust anyone; neither could I trust myself. This led me down the pathway of alcohol abuse and heavy partying. This was my coping mechanism because I just wanted to escape what I was going through. I was on the road to destruction. One day, I got tired. I decided that I wanted better. This was my turning point. *I decided!* I got down on my knees. I repented and prayed for healing and deliverance. God awakened me spiritually and gave me a new life, a new pathway, and my *true identity.* My identity in Christ was restored! He brought me out of darkness into the marvelous light! It does not matter what conditions you are in. God can deliver you out of it. You must believe that your divorce is not your final result. Sickness is not your final result. Heartbreak is not your final result. Abandonment is not your final result. Rejection is not your final result. Unmet dreams and goals are not the end of you.

The "look like situation" reveals to you the things that are not your final result. This is the lie that the enemy encourages you to identify with. He presents to you false visuals about who you are as well as your situation. If your mind is not in a proper position being completely aligned with the Word of God and positive affirmations about yourself, you will begin to believe the lies, tricks, and schemes that the enemy place before your eyes. I realized the mastermind behind every lie is the Father of Lies, the devil himself.

When you recognize the real enemy behind the lies that are put into your mind about you and where you are in life, your entire paradigm will *shift*! You will begin to discover who you are from within. Your true identity in Christ will spring forth! You will begin to believe that you *are more than a conqueror!* Your language about who you are will switch. God will allow your true identity to cause the trajectory of your *entire life* to switch and manifest into a beautiful picture that only comes from God. You will begin to find your purpose and head to destiny. You will be confident in knowing who you were before you were placed in your mother's womb.

The Bible says, "...greater is he that is in you, than he that is in the world" (1 John 4:4, KJV). This simply means that who you are is greater than the lies enemy told you about yourself. You are a fearfully and wonderfully made beautiful soul, according to Psalm 139:14. God has uniquely placed you together inside, out. There is no one else made to grace this earth like you. You were born with a gift, a skill, a talent, a weapon that only you can use that will break you away from the lies of the enemy about you and your true identity. Your identity is your mark, your brand, your stamp in which you will place on this earth. Your unique identification will break barriers, ceilings, and generational curses that have dominated your family for decades.

Your true identification will influence culture as this world has never seen because the God that is within you will empower you to slay giants and move mountains that are blocking you. God will give you the power to *grind everything that stands in your way* because you *are more than a conqueror*! You are born to be greater! Born to be better! Born to be salt and light! Born to create! Born to beat the odds! Born to change culture! Born to be wild! Born to be *yourself*! Who are you? You *are more than a conqueror!*

Lastly, to find your way back to your true identity in Christ, grab a marker and sticky notes. On each one, write down a positive affirmation or scripture of what God said about you. You may even want to go as far as grabbing a tube of lipstick and writing it down in your mirror. Plant those seeds in your mind by any means necessary. Speak those words over yourself every day. As you proceed, stand in the mirror. Look at yourself and smile as you speak your true identity into existence. Feel what you are speaking. Believe what you are speaking and watch it manifest! Your results will ultimately reflect the words in which you have spoken over yourself.

Your entire life is going to reconstruct as a result of what you have spoken. Words are very powerful, and it gives life or death to a thing. Speak life into the positive things to come. Your place in life will *shift* to a whole new place. God will cause every positive word in which you have spoken over yourself to manifest your vision, your dreams, divine connections, and the life you have always wanted to meet you right where you are. Your true identity in Christ has a built-in abundant life that is designed for you to attain happiness, health, wealth, balance, and success that will allow the glory of God to shine in the direction of others. Your true identity in Christ will also give others hope, and your hope will help set them free. This is God's plan for you. He wants to make you a walking billboard on His behalf that will cause you to draw many in your direction to want what God has for them. It starts with you finding yourself so that you can head to destiny! Remember, you *are more than a conqueror!*

Your true identity in Christ will also give others hope, and your hope will set them free.

Journal Writing Exercise

Your Identity

Name:

Date:

Life has a way of shaping us into so many things. Our beliefs, thoughts, and emotions make it real. Write down five positive things you know about yourself and five positive things about yourself that someone else has identified you as. Compare them. Then, write down one scripture from the Bible describing your identity in Christ. Affirm these scriptures in the morning before work/school and at night before bed as positive reinforcement.

5.

CODE OF CONDUCT

"Bless those who persecute you; bless and do not curse. Rejoice with those who rejoice; mourn with those who mourn... Do not be proud, but be willing to associate with people of low position. Do not be conceited"

(Romans 12:14–16, NIV).

Growing up in my grandmother's household shaped and molded my attitude, being, and behaviors later in life. She always emphasized to me the importance of how to behave at home as well as outside of our home. This very thing is known as a code of conduct. She taught me things such as to mind my manners, respect my elders, speak only when spoken to, stay in a child's place, do not wear my welcome out, and lastly, treat everybody right. I feel so blessed to have been raised in such a manner because it gave me a foundation of how I should carry myself as an adult.

Code of conduct is a rule of how you should be postured in terms of your behavior as an individual. After you have discovered who you are, you will begin to govern yourself in a particular fashion. Your behavior is a prominent part of your existence, and it will cause the new you to dominate the old you are, forming new habits, patterns, and mindsets that will determine your foundation as a person. You want to build a solid foundation by exercising a meaningful code of conduct. How you carry yourself in every environment and situation will speak volumes when you have a strong code of conduct. It will allow you to be light in dark places, positively and powerfully influencing all whom you come into contact with. Your presence will cause a paradigm shift in the mind of all of whom God calls you to connect.

As I think back over my life, I remember falling short on many occasions in terms of bad behavior. I became extremely rebellious when I entered certain environments. I became comfortable in the company of people that encouraged my rebellious ways. I was what is known as an angry bird with little to no self-control. I harbored anger, un-forgiveness, hurt, and brokenness which provoked me to flourish in making a repetition of bad decisions and accepting less than what I deserved. I had no standards for myself.

As I got older, I desired something different. I desired to change. I decided for the better this time to get up in my mind and set the change in which I desired in motion. In spite of how many times I fail, I reminded myself in the mind of my spirit of what Proverbs 24:16 said. It stated, "...for though the righteous fall seven times, they rise again" (NIV). I believe in the Word of the Lord, and it manifested. It took time, faith, patience, and growth to develop a strong code of conduct.

One day without expectancy, God changed my life. He shifted me into a different environment which placed me into the presence of a divine group of people. This place was extremely uncomfortable for me. I did not know how or what to feel. I was speechless. All I could do was sit quietly in awe of how God took me from one environment and set me in another environment that was designed to flourish me. This place was a cosmetology school. Yes! God used cosmetology school to change the course of my entire life. He used my incredible cosmetology instructor and amazing classmates to reach me. I found grace and mercy right there. My new environment motivated and challenged me to change my mindset. I began to set high standards for myself that governed my daily behaviors and attitudes. Among the many things in which I have learned in cosmetology school, I pressed hard on myself to eat, sleep, and live out the *golden rule*: "Do unto to others as you will have them to do unto you." This was important because life shaped me into something that I wasn't. I forgot how to treat people. I became selfish and bitter. The importance of the *golden rule* was for me to be reshaped from within so that I could flourish in my purpose and help others come out on the rough side of the mountain.

The Bible says in Romans 12:14, "Bless those who persecute

you; bless and do not curse" (NIV). This means when people hurt you, always stick to the code. When you are called to walk in a special purpose heading to destiny, you will begin to strongly govern yourself according to your code of conduct because you cannot afford to go back to old ways that will keep you bound. Stick to the code so that the course of your life be restored, renewed, revived, and redeemed! You will gain the power and authority that will empower you to walk tall in your home, your marriage, in your family, in your business, on your job, and in your community! "You must decide today to be the change you want to see in others," says Mahatma Gandhi. No matter where you are in your life, you can always begin again. Just stick to the code.

How you carry yourself in every situation speaks volumes when you have a strong Code of Conduct.

Journal Writing Exercise

Your Code of Conduct

Name:

Date:

How we model ourselves before people makes a statement about our character, attitude, and behavior. Write down ten high standards in which you would like to model before people. Your code of conduct becomes an extraordinary influence in your household, workplace, and community. Holding yourself accountable within your standards every day will sharpen your ability to reshape how you conduct yourself.

EPILOGUE

God's uniquely designed plan that He has for you leads to hope, abundance, and a future filled with His love, His grace, His mercy, and His favor. When you allow the Heavenly Father to come into your heart no matter where you are in your life, He will download in the mind of your spirit a God-filled vision of His plan for your life. He will lead you, step by step, when you decide to make yourself available for Him to speak your future into existence by way of His Word. He will allow you to see through His lens.

At that very moment, hope, along with His plans for you, will be conceived down on the inside of you. In due season, you will birth into the world your purpose assignment that will not only benefit you but will impact the masses, all for the glory of God. Then, you will experience the grace of God in a fresh way. God will grace you to become the truly identified individual in which He has created you to be. You will be able to live in the fullness of God's original plan, promises, and purpose according to His design for your life.

God does not promise that you will never encounter dark days and hardships, but He does promise to give you joy after dark days, and He promises to never leave you during hard times. He will be there every step of the way.

ABOUT THE AUTHOR

Andrea Hudson Johnson has been a dedicated business entrepreneur and teacher in the beauty industry for fifteen years. She is also the founder of Finding Purpose and Heading to Destiny, a non-profit organization that is designed to equip, edify, and empower individuals through biblical principles and who recognizes that they have a God-given call to purpose on their lives, all for the upbuilding of the Kingdom of God using their gifts, skills, talents, and abilities to grow and expand in all the earth.

Andrea is a God-fearing and loving wife of her caring and supportive husband, Kentrell Johnson, and together they have four beautiful sons. She is now residing in Southaven, Mississippi.